salmonpoetry

Publishing Irish & International
Poetry Since 1981

The Wounded
for the Water

POEMS BY

MATT W. MILLER

Published in 2018 by
Salmon Poetry
Cliffs of Moher, County Clare, Ireland
Website: www.salmonpoetry.com
Email: info@salmonpoetry.com

ISBN 978-1-910669-46-4

COVER ARTWORK: *Breathe* by Lloyd Meudell
COVER DESIGN & TYPESETTING: *Siobhán Hutson*

Printed in Ireland by Sprint Print

for Frank and Joe, for Ray and Ed, for Jon and Paul, for Barry, Brian, and Chris, and for all the fathers in our lives

Contents

Foreword   9

Pilot Verse   11

I

Ordeal by Water   15

II

Oceanography   31
Seborrhea   32
Behold, Here is My Mark   33
Trouble Is Easy   34
Slow Ripening Fruit   36
Paint   38
Indian Summer   39
Three Center Two Electron Bond   40
A Song After Wound Packing   41

III

Tips for Dove Hunters   45
What the Rain Will Not   47
And the Melt   49
This Tune Goes Manly   51
Of the Father   53
Shall the Good Man Teach   56
Resolve   57
On Nights When I Am My Mother   58
Repose   60
High School Reunion   61
Child's Play   63
Bully Pulpit   64

IV

Heat Index   67
L' Origine du Monde   68
Under Blue Blankets   69
Nude in a Tree   74
Winter Sessions   76
Symbols   77
Bounce   79
About the Deck   80
Toward June   81
Mulch   82

Notes   85
Acknowledgments   88
About the author   91

Foreword

Matt Miller's *The Wounded for the Water* moves through pick up trucks, "lasered off" pubic hair, Lowell bars, the missed chance of marriage in a parallel universe, and trees just right for climbing. Taking wisdom from everyone from Shakespeare to New England Football coach Bill Belichik, these poems confront the risks of friendship, the violence and comfort of family in the age of mass shootings and racist violence: a first grader "playing Lockdown," a recognition that the "Blonde, blue-eyed boys/of the world" must not "be conscripts//to miracles of hate."

The Wounded for the Water offers up many waters, and all their meanings: the "spray/pink inside a rising moon," "a Miami pool," "New Hampshire's slate Atlantic," "the wave as it curled into a fist," "a palm/ of sea," "thick silt and shorebreak," "glassy offshore tomorrows," and "scree of whitewater's roiling/gravity": "all my definitions of drown." Water here is as varied and useful as days, family, the rich variety of our lives.

With his singular voice, generous heart, and keen eye, Miller expresses tenderness for family, for friends, even for strangers barely glimpsed. These waters shift, become, help us understand toxic masculinity—"the kind of drowning/that picks fights with mothers. lovers, cops"; a daughter born "mute as a fish"; "friends, lovers, children not swimming/just thrashing in place." "Born of spirit./I know also my cells are made of water/so I will not let water be my cell." With fierce attention to sound and tradition, quoting Emily Dickinson, Joseph Conrad, and Herman Melville, Miller catalogs waters we drink from, swim in, drown in. He shows us how intimacy, family, our very vulnerabilities, can teach us "a new way to breathe." "You whisper/me to swim. You take November from me./And you are why there is any June at all."

—JILL McDONOUGH, author of Reaper

Out of the water, I am nothing.

—Duke Kahanamoku

Pilot Verse

Now to chart a way
of skinning waves,

to throw spray
pink inside a rising moon.

Now to slice beneath the bloom
of blue

and caesura from a curled
womb.

Now to be sewn in foam
and still to breathe,

to be a tongue
for slitting swells and breaks.

Now to whisper
too long into the fetch until

no breath left. Now
to feel that last pulse in the set

carve names across my back
in dim and brackish light.

Now to stitch across
all my definitions of drown.

I

Drowning is not so pitiful
As the attempt to rise.

—Emily Dickinson

Ordeal by Water

Maybe four when my father threw me
into a Miami pool, said *now swim to the side*
and talked me how not to drown.

So the first time I drowned I was seven,
a rubber raft, my cousin pulling me out
into New Hampshire's slate Atlantic,

the wave as it curled into a fist, pitched
me and I fell backward forever into a palm
of sea until I was the greenhead whose crush

was what the world wished for and I
twirled the underwater in the black
of my own shut eyes because to open

my eyes would have been to lung
the Atlantic. But in the dark I could hold
and hold my breath and never drown.

And then I found my legs and stood
in the shallow of what had swallowed.
A wig of mud crowned my head,

sand it seems I'm still scratching out
of my scalp. I may have cried, I know I shook
walking out of the waves back up

to the blankets of my mother, refusing
the water for the rest of the day. But still
I did not know what it means to drown.

II

Most spun-out drowning was south
of San Francisco, by the Pacifica pier.
I paddled out new: to that coast, to surfing,

to that water and its slab of autumn swells.
I didn't know the break or what rocks, what reefs,
what nictitating eyes might rise

from the black to grendel me beneath the roll
and roar of foam. I took off too steep, too deep
in the wave, and felt that fist again drill

then drag me over the falls and hold me,
curl me cozily, lovingly, beneath its belly,
under its teary-eyed pillow. I refused

the water again. I swam with open eyes
toward light licking pink under the foam inches
away. I opened my mouth to eat the air

when the ocean pulled me under again.
The leash. I was on a leash. I was leashed
to my board and it was being buried

by another thickgut wave, yanking me back
inside the dark. I didn't know if my eyes
were open or closed, if the circles of blue

red and green were synesthesia's gleam
of mermaid song or my skull blood
turning toxic. One last rubber armed stroke

toward the surface, and there it was.
Sirens slipped back into to their wreaths
as my lips crowned first and I gorged

on air and the California hills. Had another
wave risen from its haunches to strike,
I would have swallowed it to death.

III

There is a night at the Gaelic Club in Lowell,
stink of old Budweiser and Camel Lights,
the sweat of hate and sadness so deep

it has tides pulled by the moon. Maybe
25, I walk in and see a high school friend,
fellow football co-captain. Once, he popped

his dislocated shoulder back into the socket
between downs when we were losing
to Methuen. *Matty, kid, how you doin'?*

he says. *Let me get you a pop. How's things?*
What're you up to these days? What a day I had
down at the prison. Kiddy diddler gets a knife,

right? Starts cutting himself up in his cell
and I got to go in and stop him only he has
AIDS right, he was giving AIDS to little kids

and I'm like 'let him kill himself.' But no, me
and another guard got to put on these dog bite
suits and save him but the only way to do that

is to subdue him by which I mean beat him
down. Only he's tweaking, keeps coming and we
keep beating on him, beating the ever living

loving hell out of him. We pounded away
until he stopped squirming, stopped smiling,
until my hands stopped hurting and I was running

out of places to hit, until there was nothing left
of that sick prick but a purple bubbling.
You see what I'm saying? Want to do some blow?

We slip below the surface, a smile curling
up toward tears we can't allow, that we'll
swallow with *doin' goods* until we drown.

But I'm good, he says. *I'm doin' good.*
I come down here to have a few pops,
and wait around for that pension, right?

He laughs and I laugh. *You good?* he asks.
Yeah, I'm good, I lie and clinging to the art
of each other's lies we choke down beers.

IV

The summer Hurricane Bill threw waves
with twenty foot faces along New Hampshire's
coast, I paddled out with too much pride

and not enough board. When an outside set
monstered in I had to duck dive, duck dive
until I did not dive deep enough, the last

double overhead a dragon of time and space
exploding on my back. I was spun and bent,
whipped and bit, my arms a pair of severed claws.

Yet it wasn't bubbles I followed up
but barnacled visions of a son who'd never know
me, a daughter who would forget my voice,

a wife who'd need to hate me one day for this.
And I began to know a little bit about drowning,
the ways to drown beyond the sea.

                             We drown

as well inside the human voice that wakes us
then breaks us upon the rocks. We drown inland,
where the sea does not reach, where water becomes

a mudhut of hurt, where nights are hours that drag
on forever, nights that are my naked body
scraped across a field of cracked ice, playing rigged

games of football next to U-hauls filled with
beer kegs and frat rush boys. The kind of drowning
that picks fights with mothers, lovers, cops,

and all the friends I murdered into strangers.
The kind of drowning that folds me
into a cabinet of sleepwalking knives,

that holds a blade to my wrist in dim lit tile
of my kitchen moonlight. Drowning where I don't
know I am drowning because flesh so dry,

parched in fact, my scales falling into the sun
as I cross the desert on my belly defaced,
deflowered, and now to death devote

as worms gnaw into that constipated place
inside my spine. And when I do reach water
it is all thick silt and shorebreak, rolling me

back in, chalked in alluvium, drowning in sun,
beached, cooking in my own fat, my own blood,
the once rich oil of my skullbone rotting before

it ever could lick a candlewick. I have been
one drowning like this. I'd once wished to keep
drowning. But what did I know of drowning?

V

My daughter is born drowning, choking
on blood and amniotic fluid caught in her throat
as I stand dumb. In my hand, the scissors

that never get to cut the purple grey rope
coiled slippery between child and mother.
She does not come crying onto her stage

but rather hacking, scratching at air,
laid out on a pan, mute as a fish, by doctors
yelling for *help now, no now, yes now*.

How many times must you say *now* in a hospital?
They take her nameless into the NICU.
My wife is a web of torn tissue and tears

as a doctor digs rubber gloves back into her.
More bleeding down here than I like to see, he says.
Scissors, needle, thread now old hands snip

winces rip her face. *See if she's okay, make her
be okay*, she says and I run down a hall
as if hip deep in mud, watching walls implode,

doors blowing open into a pool of blue swimmers
too small for March and I won't feel bad hoping
my baby isn't one of them. *Now this way, Daddy*,

someone says and then her eyes open, pools
staring, and we are right there terrified, beautiful,
drowning in what the world can take,

what it will take from us breath by breath,
rubied, from systole to diastole, each pulse
a fading out of glassy offshore tomorrows.

VI

I read that the drowning are unable to call out
for help. The respiratory system was designed
for breathing. Speech is the overlaid function.

I see this also away from water. In the pitch
and swirl of day on day we watch each other
drown because drowning does not look

like drowning. It is silent. But there are signs:
head tilted back, mouth open, eyes glassy and
empty, no use of legs, gasping, trying to swim

but not making headway, appearing to climb
an invisible ladder. We've all seen this lie
of climbing: friends, lovers, children not swimming

just thrashing in place. We watch in our homes
on sidewalks, in offices, and classrooms
eyes staring out at nothing. A friend,

she's playing, tumbling in a turquoise surf,
eyes full on love's pinks and soft blue
coral and then she is pounded into the reef,

torn across its razored skeleton, spun in threads
of her own blood, her body shredding,
shredding into all the beautiful colors and I

watch, not understanding the signs when birds
begin to flee, when the sea suddenly sucks away
from her Malaysian coast. Or not understanding

the Katrinas swallowing a mother's bones,
or my wife locked in a winter tower sleepless,
hungry, with a cold lump of coal growing

in her breast as she tries to rock a screaming
cradle where our son's hurt drowns day
into night. I spin words not knowing that

I cannot see the wounded for the water.
There are bodies drowning all around me,
my mother in the dark water of an empty

home where the stench of Dad's dead man's
chest, of his bile leaking gut, still swims
as she lights scented candles in the soaked air.

Brothers, sisters, sons and daughters,
all the swollen tongues of a scorched earth,
all asking for mercy of unruly sea gods

while my hands seem too slow to let go
of the ship's brass railing, to let loose the line—
because what do I know of drowning

but that I drown dumbly in their thousand
furlongs of tears, of blood, of bile—quiet
as a breath that will not come.

VII

There is a reason why their drowning
is my own, why I waken from the dream where
again and again my son is falling off a pier

into a bottomless black and I dive in
but cannot find him for the water is too deep,
too dark. And, waking, I have to run

to him, terrified as I am by those trips
taken to the emergency room when asthma
sinks a stone onto his wheezing lungs.

There is a reason why their drowning
is my own, why in winter stripped maples
I see my father drowning for thirty hours,

unhooked from the ventilator because
he was tired of swimming against the mad
currents and sick rips of his failing flesh.

There is a reason why I drown, why at night
I wonder what my mother does to fall asleep,
to brush his bloody bandages from her eyes.

When the slope of waves becomes too great,
when all of our inertias hit the shoals,
breaking's as inevitable as froth and twirl.

There is a reason I want to drown in them,
why when I reach the NICU and see
my daughter's dark doll eyes wet, alive,

and smiling under the lights I become
liquid,
       I become water.

                And how can water
drown? How native unto that element

and fear the muddy pull?
                Born of spirit,
I know also my cells are made of water
so l will not let water be my cell.

VIII

Transferential

Because there must be other ways to drown,
ways of drowning where you do not die
or you die only to rise from the waters

baptized, washed, witness to a purged
earth. There needs a taking back of *drowning*,
a wash of drowning in new definitions,

the drowning in another's eyes and arms, drowning
in a smile, peacefully letting go in the waters
of someone else. The drowning that saves,

heals, that allows you to keep company
with hope, makes you start swimming.
Emily, sea-eyed, would have dreams

of drowning in giant waves. She tells
me this in her Brookline apartment, when we
first start dating, when I am falling in love.

So what did you do? I asked a childhood ago
I taught myself to breathe in underwater dreams,
she said. This is how she saves me

from my own drowning, not by reaching
out to pull me from my rip currents,
but by showing me that if you don't want

to drown, if you're worried about the rising
water, teach yourself, demand of yourself,
a new way to breathe. Drowning in that light

of morning, still drowning in that silt
of soft touched lips, in those sweet waters,
I took first breaths against my dry cage of ribs.

The intellectual is always showing off, writes
the Sufi poet. *The lover is always getting lost.*
The intellectual runs away, afraid of drowning.

I shall take back *drowning*. I'll drench it
in my own colors, my own algebras,
semantics, permutations of pulse and swell.

My drowning is not to be a suffocation,
but an absorption into the fickle sea,
gliding in its physics, cross-stepping its gravity,

slipping its long leash of push and pull, breathing
and sharing breath beyond the limited lining
of my lungs as I carve oxygen from a spray

of foam thrown up orange and violet
in the singing out of a sailor's evening sun.
And now I dive for the cool depths

of all my others. Adrift in the flood of her,
of our children, of you, of every you and the blue
of this deluge, I cannot have too much

of water. My sea as you are my blood,
you let me breathe in underwater dreams.
You are water in which I wish to drown,

the depths where I respire. You whisper
me to swim. You take November from me.
And you are why there is any June at all.

II

language

He had picked up enough of the language to understand the word water, repeated several times in a tone of insistence, of prayer, almost of despair.

—Joseph Conrad

Heart of Darkness

Oceanography

Old roads, crawling dusty through cracks,
between toes, between fingers, become
the sea that was us and what has become
our presence in a soft asphalt August.

Don't forget the children, you said,
before there were children in that curl
of water where waves whiplash the land.
And this is where your hands witch the air.

By definition, this should be the great
afternoon of our argument but I am alone
in a red '72 Buick that leathers in the nose
like skin left behind from a dream.

And the ocean is attacking the teeth
of the desert, trying to slap metal
from the highway. *Just give me a little
taste of your ass* it says, speaking

only when I tell it to. I am tiding out,
giving tongue to sea dunes and sage brush,
silking a red scarf around my waist,
too vain to tie knots around my eyes.

Seborrhea

Our joke, as kids, walking
winter mornings,

about falling snow, was that it was God
shaking the dandruff

from his wooly hair. And still I
behold Him harrowing

thick yellowed nails
through the milky rime

of those hoarfrost locks
just beginning to brittle.

Scratched from His scalp,
the flakes of skin

aggregated on earth
and were rolled into men,

plowed into cities,
caught on waiting tongues

of children, and swallowed
as pure as faith

or as flesh licked just long enough
to salt its own melt.

Behold, Here is My Mark

Because too dumb or too proud to ask
a doctor, trainer, coach, another player,
and enough of both to have put your elbow
through a window during a pissing match
with your dad that had too long bladdered,
you somehow convince yourself you can't hit,
with those forty-seven stitches in your arm,
on the first day of full pads football practice.
So you unscrew the mirror from the door
of your dorm room and set it on your desk.
The witch hazel already poured upon a pair
of old toe nail clippers, you prop your elbow
upon the mirror to spy the rows of sutures.
Then, in the swelter of a ninety-degree day,
as sweat drips and puddles in its own
reflection, you begin to snip and tug, one by
one, the black whiskers from the wound
that will never heal right, will always have
a fat and tender scar, and will tear open
every day for every season of that game,
in spite of all gauze, bandages, and butterflies,
and bleed and bleed, as if you had wanted it to.

Trouble is Easy

Just be a wandered off kid
at an airport and shove

your arm into the hot black gap
of space where the conveyer belt

slips back under the edge
of the x-ray machine.

Make sure you're old enough
to know this is stupid,

young enough to have an arm
that can fit through but still get stuck

as the belt starts rubbing away
layers of skin. Now you're in it.

At first, do nothing. Your mom
is wiped out already travelling

with three sons all under the age
of five from Miami to Boston.

But then you will have to scream.
It will hurt. People's luggage

will shove and knock up against you.
That's when she'll freak, your mom,

hearing you cry, seeing you sucked
down by rubber, wheels, metal.

Then the awful alarm. The lights.
The machine howling to a stop.

Somebody pulls your arm out.
There will be men in uniforms.

One will pour something stinging
onto the white pink brand you will

think looks like an eye right before
they bandage it up and help you all

to the gate before it's no longer
1978 and people start suing

over such things. Then wait
a week or so and be a royal

pain in the ass big brother
at a crowded Burger King.

Steal your brother's toy or fries,
make him screech so Mom

grabs you wild-eyed by the wrist
still wrapped in gauze and tape

and starting to yellow and stink.
Best to let her see the blood first,

after her squeeze rips the scab
and red streams through her fingers.

Then start wailing. It's still '78
so no one will call social services

and you'll get all the fries you can eat.
Plus, that look on her face.

Slow Ripening Fruit

There are three of us in the cab
of the dump truck. I'm driving.
Brian, my buddy who owns
the landscaping company, hangs
his tired right arm out the passenger
window. Frank, teeth missing
or twisted in his head, who talks
about his crack addiction,
who just got out of Billerica House
of Correction for crashing his car
headlong into a cruiser, sits
between us. *I like you guys*, he says
as we drive away from a yard,
dirt turning to dust in our eyes
and on our hands, a trailer of mowers
rattling behind us along July
baked roads of too hot Lowell.
My last job landscaping, I fucking
whacked my boss in the back
of the head with a shovel.
But he was a prick. I like you guys.
You're nice. No bullshit.
At this I look over at him and he's
staring right at me. I'm trying to see
if what he just said was
some kind of threat, a shot
across the nose to let us know not
to mess with him. But there's a tug
in his eyes, a way his glass pipe
mouth sort of hangs a bit slack
and I think, I feel, he's sincere.
Then that tug and gaped mouth
are gone. He's off on his favorite
racist joke again. But he must
have been straight when he said
he liked us because in a week or so

he will be gone, off north to Hampton
with his girlfriend and their kid
to start his own lawn crew. He must
have been on the level, to have called
us pals and then bolted, so as not to risk
a change in mood, a sudden shovel.

Paint

I do not see the spray can explode in my mother's face but I see my mother's face painted a thick and slick pitch, like some crueler sister of an Oz witch, black and glistening and horrifying. The can is already rolling away on the concrete floor, fleeing the scene, as my mother stands there blind, breathing out a slight high moan, lost between a whimper and a whine, hand stroking the muggy air around her, groping for something, someone to make this go away. My brother Jon and I start to cry but she tells us to stop, that she needs us to help her out of the garage and across the street to a neighbor's house. This is Miami and it is 1977 and I am barely four and Jon is three and we do not know anyone in the neighborhood yet, we still new from New England and our father far off on another trip for work. We take her casting hands and lead her out of the open garage like a sacrifice. Paul is the baby still napping in his crib. We have to leave him there, alone in our new house. We are not allowed to cross our street but now we have to, have to guide her to a door where she hopes someone is home. It is our first time without someone to look both ways for us and the little street seems so wide and so long. I look up at my mom and I am afraid of her, at the way the black paint shines silvery in the morning sun, off the angles of her nose and chin and cheeks and swallowing her eyelids, making her a machine of mom, a dripping Darth Vader, that summer's new monster who Jon and I saw at the movies in Lowell with Aunt Barbara while Paul was being born. And I think it is me who knocks on the door or rings the doorbell of the neighbor we do not know but whom I'd heard my mom say is a *confirmed bachelor* in a way I know there is something I do not know about the way grown-ups use words. He lets us in, he calls the paramedics, he lets my brother look at his parakeet while we wait for the sirens, while someone next door checks on the baby, while my mother tries not to cry for the pain, for her missing children right in front of her, for this city she did not want to move to, for a husband who always promises things will be different once we move.

Invasive

White moths whorl about the hot privet
        afternoon of old October as cirrus tails
rivet a venous blue sky and I try to hide

my limp until I can slip inside my house,
        grunt onto the couch, strip off my pants,
and rip off the gauze taped to my ass where

the boil has come to a head, leaks pus
        and blood across my scorched earth
of thigh. And I, I am too young for this

corruption of skin, for Sunday's pustule
        turning Tuesday's carbuncular break and burn.
I should be my ocean. I should be paddling

into a pulse of combers at Sawyer's Beach.
        My chest is still thick, my neck still thin.
And yet, at this moment, collapsing in

to my sighs, I'm bent satisfied to be
        out of the sun, away from all surf and
its sticky tongue of sand, bolted in shadows

of my den as old man afternoons begin
        barreling in, wave on wave. And then
from the sweating leather, through

the spotted glass of my bay window, watching
        autumn light slump upon a tulip tree
I see my neighbor, her hair dyed black,

walking through her garden, holding
        her pruner, kneeling into the dust
to cut the crowns from columbines.

Three Center Two Electron Bond

I sit down with the Sexiest Man Alive,
at a café in Providence of all places,
and ask him if he knows this thing about
our molecules, that they don't ever stop
moving. Even when frozen inert they're not
inert, not really. He is handsome, no doubt,
and blonde enough for today's scruffy chin
of clay. You know, though, it's his kindness
that kills me, the way he genuinely listens.
The devil is what we want of our seraphim,
not some beautiful grin buying our gins,
making it hard to be *okay looks, okay nice*
when we settle for love over money. So
I ask this guy if the molecules of his smile
will be the ones to save the universe.
His eyes mist as he says he does not think
so and then he retreats from his cosmo,
returns to his parent's tobacco farm outside
of Charlottesville. That's when he starts to call
me at night to yell about my pop mythology,
the way I rush people into icons.
Always he ends by slamming down the phone
then calling back later to say he's sorry.
I start to suspect my wife of listening in
on the other line, licking up his voice.
The Sexiest Man Alive, one night, pulls
his skin off in the thickets, brings it to auction
with his ten bushels of bright leaf.
My wife begins to travel there monthly
and smokes up everything he has, especially
his face. And now she is in the movies. You
have seen her thighs slipping over the moonlit
streets, like scissors wiping clean a scene. I guess
we never did share more than a snug covalence,
I guess my questions should have been for her.

A Song After Wound Packing

How wild this flesh can be so scalpled open,
my thigh gouged out in vivisected divot,
and that I don't exsanguinate nor begin
to right away wilt with necrotic rot.
How wild a wound can bloom red-eyed
upon external worlds, internal witness
to sun, to rain, the natural shocks. Debride
me, surgeons, open me up wide as a rose.
Make carbuncles breathe periwinkle
through this, my gape. Invade the open gate
and snip me clean with silvered scissors. Twinkle
your light into my leg. Look for a hurt
too wildfire to whittle. Stuff me with gauze.
Then needle me numb so I won't feel the flies.

III

Man, looking into the sea—
taking the view from those who have as
*   much right to it as you have it to yourself—*
it is human nature to stand in the middle of a thing
but you cannot stand in the middle of this:
the sea has nothing to give but a well excavated grave.

—Marianne Moore

Tips for Dove Hunters

A collage poem collected from *Mastering the Shotgun*,
Richard Knight, 1967

Those evenings spent autopsying
dead crows on the kitchen table
revealed much about pellet shock

and as each little songbird flew
by I would sweep each from the sky
with the kitchen whisk broom.

A shotgun wound is a hideous affair,
full of tearing and complete destruction
of tissue at close range contact—

hurts as if the very devil had bitten you—
difficult for even the most accomplished
surgeon to repair. Neighbors must

regard me with the benign
tolerance we extend toward someone
who isn't quite right in the head.

Once you learn to sweep, your wing
shooting worries are past, and shooting
will become a pleasure. If your shotgun

fits and you have the time there is no
reasonable excuse on the face
of the earth for you not to kill.

With today's modern ammunition,
plastic sleeves, ram wads, and so on
you no longer need the choking;

you can bring tragedy to your family
and someone else's. For that one reason
I did not kill a close friend this past

dove season. For a clean, humane kill,
small shot has no peer. I opened the action
and slipped a shell into the chamber.

Epilogue: I know what I set down
here is right for me. I wish I could stand
at your shoulder and help you over.

What the Rain Will Wash Out,
What the Rain Will Not

Lying in the grass,
just past the brick path

of a backyard that is ever
growing over

rose beds needing an edge,
of mulch not yet spread,

where weeds have wound
through a quarter cord of wood,

are my only daughter's
purple sneakers.

Left to last night's rain,
dark throats groan,

tongues puffed and sodden.
And pink laces, swollen

from the storm, thread eyelets
that appear to gaze at

a July sun cleaving
back shadowed morning.

Seeing the shoes, I hear
my bark breaking on her,

last night after surfing
together, after eating

ice cream in the car,
for slapping at her brother,

a boy of delicate skin and heart,
who pouts in the dirt,

a boy whose tattered shoes
my wife and I always seem to lose.

We've never had to go find
hers. She always sets them behind

the back door and not out there
in the dark of crickets, bats, thunder.

Yet there they are, in the blades
of midsummer sod,

too drenched to be brought in
to a still dark kitchen.

And the Melt

The last, or close to last, low-lit
purple mist strip club I ever
went to woke me with a phone call,

ringing in the same breath of morning
in which I'd fallen, toppled,
asleep in the Vegas Hard Rock

Hotel, my brother passed out
next to me in our shared sheets.
I flipped open my flip top and

a sugared voice asked me to come
through on a Red Bull and vodka
promise to deliver pizza

with her to her son
and his second grade class.
I talk too much at strip clubs.

I have never been comfortable
with the premise, so I ask
about hometowns, scars, kids.

She and I talked two hours
while I bought dances
so she could get paid and even

though I told her not to dance
she wanted to dance.
Years later, I don't remember

her name, but I still stare
at the mole by her lip.
Or was it by her left breast?

She laughed at the jokes we made
of ourselves. I did not go with her
that morning to pass out

slices, soda, then into her bed.
I regret the pizza. And the melt
of sugar when I said I wouldn't.

This Tune Goes Manly

A witch's tit Tuesday night and I'm on dorm duty at the
boarding school where I teach, coach, and live. If you don't
know, then don't ask, but duty in a dorm is about as fun as it
sounds. Anyway, there's a fuse blown in some boy's room and
I don't have access to the fuse box closet. This other kid needs
an escort to the health center because he's hooked on online
gaming and needs to spend a few nights away from the pipe,
so to speak. So I call campus safety. They send over an officer,
real nice guy, last name Shanahan from his badge. We get the
fuse situation settled and head over to the room of the boy
cracked up on War Craft and knock at his door. He's packing
clothes and books, says he will be back out in a few. Shanahan
and I get to talking and maybe he hears something in my
accent because he asks where I grew up. I tell him Lowell. He
says he grew up there too. He asks do I know the Owl Diner?
I say shit yeah I'm going there this Sunday with my mom since
it's been five years since my dad died and the brothers are
taking her to breakfast. I bring up Donna O' Keefe who
waitresses there, whose boys I played football with. Of course
he knows her, his dad owns the place. And he says he went to
Central Catholic and I tell him I went to Lowell High and asks
me my age and when I tell him he asks if I know Shane Norton
who went to MIT or Steve Mattheos who is now a doctor and
I say sure, they were pals with my brother. I ask if he knows
Mike Sullivan who went to Central, moved to Southie and got
a divorce. Or Chris McGuirk, whose coffin I helped carry
fourteen falls ago after he flipped his white Camaro into a
dumpster. We bang on the student's door again then talk a
little more about our kids, our jobs, and funny, ain't it, how
we both ended up here in front of this door? Then the
conversation sort of turns to sand, gets chalky, like we don't
want to push too far, find out too much. Maybe there's
violence between us, some feud unsettled, some lost or stolen
girl. Maybe we played each other one Friday night at Cawley
Stadium and didn't get payback after a cheap hit on punt
coverage. Maybe one drinking night back in high school we

stood on opposite sides of a fight, maybe with bats or maybe Laduc was there and pulled his .22 from the glove box. Maybe instead we look straight ahead upon the pale green door of a boarding school student's room, waiting to save the boy from those games that keep him up all night long, waging wars against the avatars of boys he'll never know.

Of the Father

"God is exalted in his power. Who is a teacher like him?"

—Job 36:22

I.

Wet cigar end of August, the hot
a sick fat ghost in the kitchen
where my brothers, mother, and I
sweat and wait. Paul cracks an egg
too loud for our father on the phone
and he erupts, tongue all battle
axe, eyes snorting warhorse—
yells for quiet in his home
when he is taking a work call.
We straighten into pikes,
phalanx to gut his cavalry
until Mom, chewing back brine,
screams us all out into night. I fury
through the backyard, as angry
as my father so easy to anger,
kick a ball into chokecherry
trees, and pound down our black top
to the garage, where a new pane
of glass grins in the door.
I throw a forearm shiver into the sheet,
from my elbow to my shoulder.
Oh, the way the glass gives
and keeps giving, trilling, slicing,
as it falls onto old bikes in the dark,
with such a sweet and simple hate.
My elbow, the flesh, meat and marrow,
opens to the bone, an eye, a mouth,
a surge of black and red boots.
What did you do? Jon asks, looks
at my arm and then tears toward Dad

and shoves him. Dad knocks him
to the mulch, tells me to get into the car,
packed with all my stuff.
                        We wait
five hours in the ER for the two layers
of 47 sutures. It is four a.m. when,
we check in, bandaged, still so stinging
to the touch, to the hotel a block
away from my first day of college.
It is three hours before he will weep
on the sidewalk outside the dorm
and say *I'm so sorry I fucked this up*,
when I will look down at the chestnut
of his business cut, and see, as if suddenly,
that I am inches taller than him.

II

Last night, the pulse of anger, I grabbed
my daughter and struck her. Her cheek,

a rap of fingers really, bruises there not there
which I can't undo as I leave her to the darkness

of her room. Then I moved through sadness
at what she'd done, wept to my wife that I'd lost

the little girl of Purple Blankie, of Bitty Baby,
who giggle-tackled me in the dry California grass.

Today, we kick a soccer ball back and forth
and I ask her, my daughter, about that word.

Does she know what it means, why it might
be wrong for her to scratch it with a stone

upon the wall of the school where I teach
poetry, writing, language, irony.

Do you know what it means? How it means?
When it hurts and when it is just

the right word to say, shout, at times in hate,
often in joy? Do you know the bonfire it ignites?

Have you heard of a bird, the kestrel, called
windfucker, who flies against the breeze?

That the word was a word meaning to strike?
Do you know now the word (sometimes) means sex?

She doesn't really get it, but nods when I ask,
You've heard it said before and wanted

to play with it, to see it pour from your own fingers?
Words have power, don't they? I ask and

she mumbles a yes. *But if you don't know the word*
and what it can do, you lose control

of that power, like letting loose a swallowing
storm. Do you see that now? Yes, she did see,

last night, crying in the dark, she saw the storm
that swallows, that bellows. That strikes.

Shall the Good Man Teach

This week I've walked to work with gravel
still grinding in my neck from forgotten tackles
and my mind on my son, wondering if his body
will be safe, if somehow playing catch catches
fire for him and he signs up for helmets and pads,
his bones, his brain, his spine on the scrimmage
line. All the while I've ignored what a father
should not, his soul. But then all over the news:
big men, big as the abstraction of barbarian
invasions, are blitzing their thickened thumbs
toward each other, calling each other faggot
and bully, nigger and redneck. Their tweets
are the birdsongs mouse might hear before
shrike spears him on the thorns. Media pimps
debate between what's a punch, what's a tickle.
So the mean of pro linemen becomes a headline
about man's measure in a land where the rituals
to manhood are boys martyred on six man sleds
on August afternoons. Who here's a hero and what
makes a coward lathers in the tailgates, on call-in
talk shows, in locker rooms, in the proud quiet
between fathers and sons on Friday night truck rides
home from last play wins under thousand watt lights.

Resolve

"Before he shot himself fatally in the chest Thursday, the former Chicago Bears defensive back Dave Duerson sent family members text messages requesting that his brain tissue be examined for the same damage recently found in other retired players."

—New York Times, 2/19/2011

Of course, there is a risk,
putting muzzle to a chest
layered with bone, flesh,

muscle hardened by metal,
that even at high caliber
the bullet won't strike true,

may not slip the ribs, or may
pass through too clean
to rip lungs, tear spine,

and so you're left a bleeding
broken husk, dying but not
dead, the only thing left

in those final seconds,
those last eternities, the head,
where you've ached for years

to shove that bullet, to drill
through the poisoned stone,
to quiet the howl, to collapse

that cave of ink and ice
into which the sick wolf
has been dragging you.

On Nights When I am My Mother

after Meg Day

I have still not drifted to the center
of our California King as I lie awake, wondering
if that bellowing belly, those deep brown
eyes, that smile that could con the devil,
my husband, who died ten years ago,
after his seven years slow withering,
whether he loved me or just the presence
of me, the role of me going to Marshall's
to clothe the kids for school, cutting the lawn,
or having it cut, meeting with teachers,
filling the fridge, especially with ice cream
for when he'd be home on Sundays
and I'd take the boys to Matthew's Church
as he'd lay in bed watching Bonanza reruns.
I wonder did I love him. And when I joke
to my sons that my first sleepover away
from home was my honeymoon I laugh
but suck back a breath and wonder
if that is why I married him. On nights when
I am my mother, I can still see him cigarette
thin in the face of my football coach father
in the soft lit and warm kitchen I grew up in
asking my father for my hand. My father
has just said he's not impressed and the man
I will marry says he's not there to impress
him. On nights when I am my mother, I hope
the boys will bring the kids by, that my oldest
will not be so short with me in the same way
the man I married was. On nights when I am
my mother, I am sorry that I am a fool
to my son who does not know what
it feels like to everyday debride a wound that
will not heal in a sucking, sunken stomach.

On nights when I am my mother, I wonder
if I should have made them help me change
their father's dressings, clean the blood, pus,
shit, and piss from the sheets. No, I did not
want to take that much of their father away
from them. No, I am not a fool. They are
becoming better fathers than he was, perhaps,
but on nights when I am my mother, I don't
like the way they bark, sometimes, at their wives.
On nights when I am my mother, the broken
flesh that is still my husband asks me
for more pain medication and I say yes and
he asks for more and I give him more,
so a little extra oxy drips through his j-tube.
On those nights, I remember the way we looked
at each other that day we went to the pain
management doctor who told him, *I don't even know
how you are alive* and for the first time he wept
for the long days of hurt still to come. So when
the man I married looks at me, says a little more,
I love him, and so I do. And when, again, paramedics
show up to revive him, when our boys arrive,
terrified to hold his withered hands, when they leave
because they have the luxury to leave, when we
are alone again in his sleepless moaning nights
and he says more without saying more, I know
that he is my husband, that he loves me, knows me
enough to know that I will, that I am, always, more.

Repose

*for Noah Pozner, one of the 20 children murdered
at Sandy Hook, 12.14.2012*

The boy, age six, wearing a fur collar
bomber jacket, in a photo sent to the news,
grins red licorice lips under a shock
of chocolate that needs to grow in more.
I cannot wipe this photo from my mind,
cannot stop looking it up online, terrified
it might be gone, terrified that it still
remains. This boy, at only six, knows
how to cock his head back to smile,
inviting other people inside that smile.
Maybe in this he mimics dad, maybe Mom.
I look up his birthday. He's barely six
in the photo. He flutters fairy wing lashes
just like the lashes of my son, almost four.
The boy wears a jacket Mom maybe bought
for first days of fall, probably at TJ Maxx,
maybe the Gap. Weeks after his death,
his mom will dream she dropped a baby
from a mountain. She talks about this
in an interview. And she recalls her boy,
just six, wandering downstairs one night,
for one more hug, his pajama top off so
I can, he said, *feel your heartbeat better.*
My daughter is seven when she sees
the shot of the boy in a bomber jacket, who,
a month past six, will be shot eleven times
at close range, that smile torn away
with his jaw, his left hand too mangled
to hold an angel stone in his casket.
She, his mother, knows her son, only six,
is owed a reckoning so will ask that it,
the casket, be left open

High School Reunion

The cheap cocktails smudge the lens and
cudgel open a soft heart of skull

where once a rope swing in the elm, the river, the grill
bumped over at a barbeque,

where once toy tanks in the tall grass, little league
bubble gum, dusty August onion

rings, once itchy underpants, a note dropped, locker
combinations, slow walks holding

hands, growing up into crowbars and bats in the gas
station parking lot, the one .22 in the glove

compartment of a '78 Nova rusted blue with a hole
in the floor and a stolen tape deck

stereo of stone wash, Champion sweaters, hair
waiting in a can, masturbation

discussed in a city bus not long after
a bomb scare, teachers creeping on pretty track

stars so cold, wonderful, Bud Light bright
the complete devotion to the tears and the play

of furious cliché blocked, propped,
and costumed in real time across a script

a century or so old in the woods
behind the football field, in the cement

factory, by the train dodge train
tracks doing push ups for the cops lining us up

for the wagon and phone calls home
for which we will now wait up all night one

blue October after our electric
archetype has long slipped behind an iris wipe.

Child's Play

You hear your son—your first grader,
who will help a classmate put on her coat

and not yet be troubled by the teasing
of other boys, who's so afraid of ghosts

he needs his sister's jokes so not to quail
at Casper, who still labializes all his r's,

who has eyelashes of upswept gossamer—
as he plays with his plastic dinosaurs

in the back of your pick up, wail a siren
sound over and over. And it is this noise

that nudges you from a din of sports radio
to ask him what game he is playing.

He tells you he's playing Lockdown.
Your ribs heave with a sudden breath,

fissures tear across your chest, as if ripping
out a line of stitches. *We practice at school,*

he says. When you ask him if it's scary
he says, *No, but it can be uncomfortable*

*when we all have to crouch in that dark
corner. The teacher puts colored paper*

on the door window, he says. You ask why.
So the robber in the hall cannot see inside.

Bully Pulpit

Blonde, blue-eyed boys
of the world, confess

our sad bones to each other—
do not be conscripts

to miracles of hate. You must
know our handsome

is a lie, a confusion of place,
of time, of the eye—

nothing but a pop fly lost
in the sun, suddenly caught

in a stiff leather mitt, by a blind
stab at the sky.

IV

The sea had jeeringly kept his finite body up, but drowned the infinite of his soul. Not drowned entirely, though.

—Herman Melville

Heat Index

And so bird jumps inside cricket,
the music of their rubbed dawn
slides along soft blacktop corners
where summer likes to sit and stew.

Somewhere, guitar strings,
greasy as afternoon underwear
on a Sunday like this, play a kind
of slutty syrup of chords until

swallowed by the sudden hunger
of a lawn mower. December's out there,
lurking in the steamy breath of old
growth elms gone weary

and too wilting to abbreviate
the howls of turtles and dogs.
But for now, there is no air to kiss
the scrim of sweat. And the children,

drowsy blue from a dream
of rain, their cheeks sticky stained
by swirls of soft serve, wrinkle
the linen of a too early moon.

L'Origine du Monde

after the painting by Gustave Courbet, 1866

It's like a Slip 'n Slide down there, says a friend
about his wife who had the hair around her vulva
lasered off. *Now she's clean cut as any porn star
or ten-year-old girl.* That unfortunate pairing aside,
this trend is ubiquitous: to hack back jungled earth,
brushfire the downy deltas and strip mall islands
where birds emerged and still need to nest. Now
Baubo's joke's cut short, Keats' grot a public fountain.
A Slip 'n Slide, I think. Some kid's summer toy—
one that's good for about a day or two and then
it tears and leaves you wanting for what you left,
wishing for ocean, for beach, and for grassy dunes.

Under Blue Blankets

You're straight, right? says a lean black man
in a sub shop on Mass Ave

by the Orange Line stop as you fill up
a cup with ice and Sprite.

Yes, you say before the question
has really set in right,

before you have had time to consider
other answers, other possibilities.

You are 23, from a mill town,
you played ball, you like breasts and ass

but perhaps there is a wonderful other
world to love,

to hug, to press lips to lips and linger
at the luxury of a kiss.

What a waste, he says and smiles and turns
to the door, a bike at his side, a Coke

in his long fingered hand.
And was it a waste? Was there a moment

you should have walked after him,
asked him, *Why, why a waste?*

And maybe you walk a few blocks
with him and maybe you don't

go back to work that day but grabbed
a beer at Bukowski's

and maybe you go
back to his place, feel a hand

slide up your thigh. Or maybe
you wait a couple of days and

then go back to his place.
Maybe his is a kiss

you never knew existed, a kiss
that touches a different type of tender.

Maybe he shows you the gentle
in a man's thick hands,

thighs. And maybe you always wanted
a hug as hard as your own

and so you talk to your girlfriend,
your mom, your dad, your brothers.

Years will need to happen until
the two of you eat turkey and gravy

with them but it will happen,
and the two of you will buy flatware

and build shelves in an apartment.
And you'll try to write as he gets up

to go to work. *Children? I don't know.*
We start that talk but never

finish. We drink wine, The Walking Dead
is on, and we joke sad and silly

about the zombie straight.
He will have taught me to love his beard,

his stink after a workout. Does he want more?
Does he want a nice house in JP?

We enjoy cliché, think it so kitsch. We laugh
at ourselves but kiss deep

after the vows in Cambridge
on that wonderful summer Sunday.

What will he be doing? A waiter?
An architect? A fire fighter. Yes, a fire fighter,

Engine 28 and he stays strong and lean
but lets me get fat filling out

forms for fellowships so I can write
the books that no one buys.

Why not a novel, like the one
Sheryl wrote? Now she's on TV

and you are so much cuter than she is
but the way he says it is somehow

not as true as it once was. *I'm not*
so cute as those cuddling moments

in the bedroom we shared that winter
we couldn't pay for heat

so we rubbed calves together
under baby blue blankets and at *baby,*

as I retell that story, I balk
and he pretends not to notice. I say

something about kids again and he says
he wants to go out. *Let's go out,*

we never go out and I say, *You go.*
I have edits to do. And he does and comes

home late and smells of someone else
but you don't ask because, well,

because you should have gone out.
You never go out and the way he lies down

with his back to your back hurts, hurts
deeper than anything you've ever known

because something has turned, something
cold kicks in the blue blankets

even as he whispers something
about adoption before passing out

in the musky darkness. In the morning
you go out alone to a diner

to get eggs and coffee and you see
the girl you dreamed about one night

in college, a dream you did not realize
you remembered until you see her.

In the dream she had on a red sweater
and black jeans and here she is, black jeans,

red sweater. Her eyes hold yours.
You don't drop them like you always do.

She will look at you with a smile that crushes
you like a stepped on roach. You talk and joke

about things you knew and all the things
since. You feel this pulling in your arms,

shoulders, a desire to touch her cheek,
her hair, as if you had done so

a million times before, something old
and familiar and you see it cross her eyes too

for just a second. Then it's gone. You ask
if she's still married and maybe she's divorced

but the kids are great and maybe she asks
about him and you say, *Yes.*

She jokes and says, *What a waste,*
and she'll laugh and you'll laugh too.

You exchange numbers but will never call.
You go home and he is waiting.

I'm sorry, he says. *I'm sorry too.*
And then the clumsy kiss, goofy hug.

He makes lunch and you talk,
you talk like we haven't talked in years.

Nude in a Tree

Strange land behind the eyes,
or some unsettled thing in the wind,

a vision of my wife, shoeless,
stepping over the October grass

of our backyard. I watch her
behind the thin red curtain

of our bay window.
She ghosts into the tangle

under the old growth elm,
stares into the tree's grey, its leafless

and withering gnarl. And then
she embraces it and begins

to climb, as sure as a child.
She works her way up and, near

the top of the last branch thick
enough not to break, she strips.

First, her sweater. Then her blue
bra. Her small breasts pale

the purpling sky. She slips
off her jeans and panties, sliding

her thighs with the limb to wiggle
them down to one ankle where they

dangle a second before she kicks
them to the undergrowth.

She presses her face to the elm,
her eyes closed, arms cradling.

Her knees gently grip,
flesh flush with bark.

A lace of wind rocks the limb
and I watch the dusk deepen

around a congruence—of sky
and tree, of breeze and she.

Winter Sessions

The thin guitarist with chickens
in a backyard pen breathes
over the steaming cup of green tea
toward his student, tells her finger
the pick as if upon a trigger, tells her
to strum not pluck or pull against
the strings. No, keep it smooth, he says,
in a voice all timbre of September.
She is anxious, her hands like hams
she thinks, as she cross picks chords,
moves up and down a D minor root.
Something like music leaks from her
beat up Bristol, swirls in the teacher's
den between the bang on bad strings
and the creak of wooden chairs.
The thin guitarist nods, plays
along, not smiling, not frowning,
lost in listening to notes folded
together. She will never be great.
Hers will not be fingers the world
will bray about. Sill, one night far away
she will play in her kitchen, in some
city far away from backyard chickens.
Alone, she'll strum a song for a man
or a woman. She will remember
for a moment the guitarist's regard
for the notes she played well,
the ones she missed, the way winter
afternoons the two of them just sat,
a coffee table between them, and loved
that such terrible things as we, who
tear at each other for flesh, for fire,
can divine such beauty by flat picking
metal guts to make them rhyme.

Symbols

I have these two friends so in love
with football, the NFL,

that one even crushes
hard on Gronk and both are blown

away by what happened with Hernandez
and they eat up all

the it is what it is of Coach's
press conferences. But beyond

TB12's dimple, it's the physical
skill and the pitch of the emotional

that enthralls them, that makes them
sleep like the sick

when the Pats drop a game
to the *fuckin' Jets.* These two friends

lean back on lawn chairs, tailgating
with my wife and me

one autumn Sunday at Gillette.
Sitting close, smiling into the sun,

they sip the whiskey cocktails
that the one of them that is

a bartender has made for us.
And they eat up all

the grilling flesh over which I hover
my thin steel spatula.

Goatees in team gear, with no necks,
park pick-ups around us,

kettled bellies laughing, slapping,
pulling handshakes into knuckled hugs,

ass-grabbing in the stubbled light.
Mesquite and cigar smoke

cloud in the rolling pearls
of sweat upon these men's heads

for today, in this lot, they can be
men, loud and happy and drunk

on beer, on each other, on lines
so clearly chalked. My friend who

bartends touches the shoulder
of her wife, says, *This is just a symbol,*

then pulls her hand away,
as if from a center's thick thighs.

A touch, a look, all they will,
right now need, to push upon this field.

Then they return to laugh, to drink,
and eat up all this us

before we rise to join
in singing our national anthem.

Bounce

Do bad guys like trampolines? my son asks.
A throw away question, perhaps,
one in a long row on a winter afternoon.
But it has me on the hip to imagine

some Iago let go his grip to bounce
his heart upon his sleeve and tumble
with no monster in his thought.
Nor can I see the Joker, now the bad guy

on our balance sheet after America's
century of grins, rather than watch
worlds burn, flop into a flip and laugh,
really laugh, which is to say, at himself.

And could Milton's fork-tongued frat boy,
sufficient to have stood, be free to fall again
on his ass, tumble a happy field, know bliss
upon bliss? Ahab perhaps would wobble

on his whalebone, but to be silly-willing
might risk much more than a fate turned
round and round like yonder windlass.
No, it's for the trample, not trampolines,

that our bad guys leap. They don't whirl,
Joe, can't twirl, won't grin a goofy landing,
like you will, Joe, your blond hair so soft
and so spiked in the electrified air.

About the Deck an Idiot

but bivouacked in this sea, set upon an egg, its single fin set up just right for carving these shoulder high lefts, he wades the is of was and will be.

Summer slips the moon its light. August's old lobster boats putter across an eastern scrim of night that is blue stone dissolving in old bone Atlantic.

To eyes bent west, the sun sets fat in the dunes, cottages, and marshes, tossing its billion embers into foam. He bobs hip deep between this fire, that gloam.

Waves like wine glasses mouth wishes and, burnished in the sunset, score a pink so sore distinct from the night behind. Waiting for a set, he stares

into eternity's roll inside those fragile hollows. And then a billow peaks. He turns, paddles languidly from the scree of whitewater's roiling

gravity until board and he gut the earth, both yanked into a pull of birth. Everything is easy, as if falling down a dream. He pops up, clumsy feet

gripping the wax. The sandbar bores its curl into the brine. He tucks into flickers of time, dry ticks in the barrel. And then the eye upon his babble

winks, the green room closes the door, the ceiling sinks. He cannot crouch out. Arms fail and back bends. He flails, stumbles again. Any world watching

watches him thrown into spit of rose and milk. For all his able, for all his struggle to stand against the fall or fall again to stand, for all the universe there

he scans, he goes about the deck an idiot. But bivouacked in this sea, paddling back into the deep's horizon, he wades the is of was and will be.

Towards June

On the bone and crust of melting
snow, in the first warm sun of March,
a man, fat and bald, has a smoke
on the sidewalk outside his tenement
housing. He wears no shirt. His body
hair reaches from back to belly and
over the pale meat of his shoulders.
And he is beautiful, defiant, as if
his every last follicle slips a new shoot
through winter's cold clapboard grin.

Mulch

Now day turns ever November
as the schoolyard iron

and plastic of slides, rings,
ladders, and bars

stab into the backfat
of grey sky and the children

dropping in play upon the mulch
will be mulch themselves

to one day enrich the soil.
This seems as much of earth

as we will ever be,
a skinny quilt of bark

and leaves until we bark
and leave inside tin can

songs of winter.
And yet there is more.

Must be more. Even sour
breath suggests a sweet

that will come, or has.
Something yet warm and wet

breathes between an earth
and sun ever in vine

towards each other. Even
as we are blanket to autumn

bulbs, a thing to soften
the blows of falling children,

even then, the lilac's death
must doctrine existence.

Notes

p. 11 "Pilot Verse" Pilot verses were sailing directions sung to popular tunes. This was a handy way to memorize crucial navigation information: http://shanty.rendance.org/lyrics/pilot_verses.php.

p. 16 "Grendel" from the Old English epic poem *Beowulf.*

p. 16 "teary eyed pillow" is a loose allusion to *Othello* and the pillow Othello used to suffocate Desdemona in Act 5, scene 2.

p. 19 "clinging to the art of each other's lies we choke down beers" is an allusion to *Macbeth*, Act 1, scene 2: "As two spent swimmers that do cling together/And choke their art."

p. 20 "my arms a pair of severed claws" and "inside the human voice that wakes us then breaks us upon the rocks" are allusions T.S. Eliot's "The Love Song of J. Alfred Prufrock": "I should have been a pair of ragged claws/ Scuttling across the floors of silent seas" and "Till human voices wake us, and we drown."

p. 21 "defaced, deflowered, and now to death devote" quoted from Milton's *Paradise Lost* Book 9, line 6.

p. 22 "She does not come crying onto her stage" an allusion to *King Lear*, Act 4, scene 6: "When we are born, we cry that we are come/To this great stage of fools."

p. 23 "the drowning are unable to call out/ for help. The respiratory system was designed/ for breathing", "drowning does not look like drowning," and "appearing to climb an invisible ladder" from Mario Viitone's website, *Drowning Doesn't Look like Drowning* http://mariovittone.com/2010/05/154/.

p. 23 "when the sea suddenly sucks away/from her Malaysian coast." is an allusion to the Thailand Tsunami in 2004.

p. 26 "How native unto that element /and fear the muddy pull?" is an allusion to Ophelia's drowning in *Hamlet* Act 4, scene 3: "As one incapable of her own distress,/Or like a creature native and imbued/ Unto that element."

p. 28 "The intellectual is always showing off, writes/ the Sufi poet. The lover is always getting lost. / The intellectual runs away, afraid of drowning," quotes a poem by Rumi.

p. 28 "You take November from me" is an allusion to *Moby Dick*, chapter 1: "Whenever it is a damp, drizzly November in my soul; whenever I find myself involuntarily pausing before coffin warehouses, and bringing up the rear of every funeral I meet; and especially whenever my hypos get such an upper hand of me, that it requires a strong moral principle to prevent me from deliberately stepping into the street, and methodically knocking people's hats off - then, I account it high time to get to sea as soon as I can."

p. 33 "Behold, Here is My Mark" is from Job 31:35: "Oh that I had one to hear me! Behold, here is my mark; Let the Almighty answer me! And the indictment which my adversary has written."

p. 36 "Slow Ripening Fruit" is from Aristotle, "Wishing to be friends is quick work, but friendship is a slow ripening fruit."

p. 40 "Three Center Two Electron Bond" is an electron-deficient chemical bond where three atoms share two electrons. The combination of three atomic orbitals form three molecular orbitals: one bonding, one non-bonding, and one anti-bonding (*Wikipedia*).

p. 40 "The Sexiest Man Alive" is an annual feature of *People Magazine*.

p. 41 "Natural shocks," from *Hamlet*, Act 3, scene 1: "the thousand natural shock that flesh is heir to."

p 45 "Mastering the Shotgun" – all words and phrases collected and collaged from *Mastering the Shotgun*, Richard Knight, 1967.

p. 51 "This Tune Goes Manly" is from *Macbeth* Act 4, Scene 3.

p. 56 "Shall the Good Man Teach" is from *Henry V*, Act IV, scene 3.

p. 74 "strange land" is a reference to Todd Hearon's poetry collection *Strange Land* and Psalm 137.

p. 77 "Gronk" is New England Football player Robert Gronkowski, "Hernandez" is New England Patriots player Adam Hernandez arrested and tried for murder, "coach" is New England Football coach Bill Belichik, "TB12" New England Patriots quarterback Tom Brady.

p 79 "Joker" is the villain from the *Batman* comic books and films, trademark DC comics, "fork tongued frat boy" is a reference to John Milton's Satan from *Paradise Lost*, "Ahab" refers to Captain Ahab from Melville's *Moby Dick*.

p. 80 "About the Deck an Idiot" is a phrase borrowed from Melville's *Moby Dick*: "By the merest chance the ship itself at last rescued him; but from that hour the little negro went about the deck an idiot; such, at least, they said he was. The sea had jeeringly kept his finite body up, but drowned the infinite of his soul. Not drowned entirely, though. Rather carried down alive to wondrous depths, where strange shapes of the unwarped primal world glided to and fro before his passive eyes; and the miser-merman, Wisdom, revealed his hoarded heaps; and among the joyous, heartless, ever-juvenile eternities, Pip saw the multitudinous, God-omnipresent, coral insects, that out of the firmament of waters heaved the colossal orbs. He saw God's foot upon the treadle of the loom, and spoke it; and therefore his shipmates called him mad. So man's insanity is heaven's sense; and wandering from all mortal reason, man comes at last to that celestial thought, which, to reason, is absurd and frantic; and weal or woe, feels then uncompromised, indifferent as his God."

p. 80 "egg" is a type of surfboard shape, a fun and forgiving shape.

Acknowledgments

I wish to thank the editors of the following journals in which these poems originally appeared, often in different form:

"Bully Pulpit" and "Pilot Verse"—*The Tupelo Quarterly*

"Seborrhea"—*Birmingham Poetry Review*

"Paint"—*32 Poems*

"Shall the Good Man Teach"—*The Florida Review*

"Symbols"—*The Southwest Review*

"Slow Ripening Fruit"—*Naugatuck River Review*

"Behold, Here is My Mark"—*The Missouri Review*

"Under Blue Blankets"—*Booth: A Journal*

"Three Center Two Electron Bond"—*Bellevue Literary Review*

"Tips for Dove Hunters"—*The Found Poetry Review*

"Of the Father"—*DMQ Review*

"Nude in a Tree" and "Incision"—*The Boiler*

"Heat Index"—*Briar Cliff Review*

"Repose"—*The Southeast Review*

"Resolve" and "'L' Origine du Monde"—*Profane Literary Review*

"Trouble Is Easy"—*The Mom Egg*

"Invasive" and "On Nights When I Am My Mother"—*Bird's Thumb*

"Of What the Rain Will Not"—*Crab Creek Review*

"And the Melt" and "Winter Sessions"—*drafthorse*

"This Tune Goes Manly"—*River Styx*

"Oceanography"—*Switchback*

"Mulch"—*Salamander*

"Ordeal by Water"—*Iron Horse Literary Review*

"Bounce"—*Breakwater Review*

"High School Reunion"—*crazyhorse*

"Child's Play"—*The Adroit Journal*

"About the Deck an Idiot"—*The New Guard: Literary Review*

I would like to thank Maggie Dietz, Todd Hearon, Ralph Sneeden, Willie Perdomo, Mercy Carbonell, Jill McDonough, Sarah Anderson, Brooks Moriarty, Brandon Courtney, Meg Day, William Brewer, Malachi Black, LS McKee, George David Clark, Gail Mazur, Michael Bazzett, Caitlin Pryor, Peter LaBerge, Gary Leising, and all the others too many to name for their support and love in the writing of this book. Thanks to Ellen Wolff, Nat Hawkins, Kelly Flynn, Sue Repko, and Johnny Griffith for all those talks on the second floor of Phillips Hall.

Thanks to everyone connected to The Sewanee Writers' Conference for that life changing experience and also to the students, staff, and faculty of Phillips Exeter Academy for their support and inspiration.

Thank you to Jessie and Siobhán at Salmon Poetry for bringing this book to life.

And all my love, all my gratitude, and all of my world for Emily, Delaney, and Joseph.

MATT W. MILLER was born and raised in Lowell, Massachusetts and is the author of *Club Icarus*, selected by Major Jackson as the 2012 Vassar Miller Poetry Prize winner, and *Cameo Diner: Poems* (Loom Press). He has published poems and essays in *Slate*, *Harvard Review*, *Narrative Magazine*, *Notre Dame Review*, *Southwest Review*, *crazyhorse*, *Third Coast*, *The Rumpus*, and *The Adroit Journal,* among other journals. Winner of the 2015 River Styx Microfiction Prize and Iron Horse Review's 2015 Trifecta Poetry Prize, he is the recipient of a Wallace Stegner Fellowship in Poetry from Stanford University and a Walter E. Dakin Fellowship in Poetry from the Sewanee Writers' Conference. He teaches English at Phillips Exeter Academy and lives in coastal New Hampshire with his wife Emily and their children, Delaney and Joseph.

Photograph: Joseph F. Lambert

www.**salmon**poetry.com

"Like the sea-run Steelhead salmon that thrashes upstream to its spawning ground, then instead of dying, returns to the sea – Salmon Poetry Press brings precious cargo to both Ireland and America in the poetry it publishes, then carries that select work to its readership against incalculable odds."

TESS GALLAGHER